THE RHYTHMS OF TWILIGHT

A COLLECTION OF POEMS

PIUS

This book is dedicated

To my Grandmother,

The most fierce and selfless woman I know, who taught me to -

Love and Live!

Contents

Contents

Contributors

Edited by Paula Shene/Tilak Dhiman

Layout by Tilak Dhiman/Paula Shene

Cover Design by Tanya Wadhwa/Tilak Dhiman

Tea Luck Publishers

33 Locust Ave, Southampton, New York

tealuckpublishers@gmail.com

1. Angelic Mates

As helpless nomads we walk,
Wandering around, from city to city
Looking for your shoulder
To rest our heads
And hearts for a bit,
All this time we forget to notice you
Hide your wings right beneath!

2. Bare Skin Whims!

Someday I shall write a poem for you
On your bare skin,
Someday I shall remember
The scent of your bosom
Embalming my succulent lips,
As the night passes through
Its darkest path.
Someday I shall forget when day would start and
Night would end.
Enchanted in thy midst
Entwined in thy fragrance
Someday I shall write a poem on your bare skin.
Someday I shall hold onto you, my ode,
All through the darkest of nights!

3. The Candle Flame!

Let that fire burn through the candle stand,
Till the wind chimes dance
To the tunes of the monsoon breeze,
Let that fire burn through the candle stand,
Till the first drops of the mango rains
Kiss the parched fragments of the earth,
Let that fire burn through the candle stand,
Until the thunderous storms wash away
My memories of you that etched across my burning skin,
Let that fire burn through the candle stand,
As it burns for you, through memories of me!

4. Drunken Souls and Drunken Dreams

Come hither, lest not worry
And despair of the cold desert night,
The drunken souls tread in the empty search
For endless casks of wine,
Quenching their thirst for intoxication,
Yet engulfing their souls with misery.
Come hither to me O' beloved,
Let us watch the dark knights' ride
Right across the skies,
As the comets that one may see once in their lifetime,
Hold me close and walk with me,
This desert is mine,
And I want to share it with thee!!

5. Ephemeral Romances!

I smile with you now; I dream of us together.
Someday when it's no longer a dream,
I will stand, far away,
Just holding onto those memories,
As you would still be his
And he would yours.
I would slowly fade away
Into the horizon,
Having no one beside me,
But just whims that went astray!

6. Faded

I'm fading through time,
My shadow disappears into the oblivion
As the dawn breaks across the desert sky
And embraces a new day,
Will I wake up to see a new dawn?
Or will I fade away with the morning breeze?
Will I ever hear the wind chimes
And sing in rhythm
As I walk through the raked-up autumn leaves?
Or will I remain a memory?
From Today,
Until eternity!

7. Footprints!

We both are mere footprints in the sand,

Across a faraway Shore,

Indelible as it may Seem,

The waves did come and take us away,

All that remain are memories,

That the waves bring back,

Each time they reach the shore,

Reminding us, of the time,

When I wrote your name with mine!

8. Ill Fated Faith

If someday in this time,
He would once again walk the face of the earth,
Would we stand in line to just see?
Myriads of us flocking by
For just a glimpse.
Or would we laugh him off as we did before
And continue killing in His name?
We killed him once for our Faith,
Why wouldn't we just do it again?

9. Just the One Time!

Kiss me, just one time,
In a way that the world
May never know.
Touch me, just the one time,
In a way that the world
Would never see.
Caress me, just the one time,
In a way that the world
Would never feel,
Lay beside me, just the one time,
In a way that the world
Would be right there with you and me.
Let's look up to the sky my beloved,
And talk to each star,
If you listen intently,
They will tell you a story of their own.

10. Mirages

Until Oblivion I walk through this lonely night,
And all I see is You,
Until dawn, I search for the desert light,
And all I see is you,
Until the depth of the ocean,
I sink tonight,
And all I see is you,
Until the eclipse breaks my sight,
All I see is you,
Until Eternity I breathe,
And all I breathe is you,
Let my eyes adorn thee,
As all I wish to see is You.

11. My Morning Prayer

Give me one morning,
So that I can wake up before sunrise
And stand by the window,
Watching the morning rays play peekaboo
With your skin,
Give me a space beside your bed,
So that I can stay up late,
To dance with you and gaze at the stars
Those only shine after midnight,
Give me some room in your home,
So we can stay warm through the winter nights,
Naked and wrapped in a soft rug.
Wake up in a room with me,
So I can write on your bare back,
That dreams do come true,
When it's about me and you!!

12. Oblivion & Beyond!

We all tend to feel oblivion,
At times when the sands just speak
In tongues of yesteryear,
We tend to feel oblivion,
We tend to touch the horizon.
We tend to defy humanity!
Until the sand passes by!

13. Pearl Showers!

The rain of pearls that crumble down the sky,
That stitches a robe all over you,
And quenches the thirst of your tender skin,
The very skin that shines in the
Vibrant colours of the first rainbow of spring,
Let those pearls come down upon you,
And paint for me a picture of how the gods see you,
When they see you from above!!

14. Secrets

My heart is a secret,
A secret within a secret,
Embedded within the Dark Abyss is the scent of you,
The Fragrance of your hair, your skin
And the warmth of your eyes,
You remain the deepest secret in me.
You remain the deepest treasure that I own.
You remain within me,
Today, Tomorrow and till the moment,
Time ceases to exist!

15. Sensual, Solemn Mysteries!

When I do make love to you someday,
I will gently hold you back
From the whistling wind,
And Grab you by the waist
And turn you right into me,
Standing right beneath the starry skies,
A sky with the bright light of shooting stars,
Wishing that this could be,
What Layman calls as our Eternity!

16. Sublime Explosions!

Explode all over me
When I'm there beneath you,
Until the burning embers
That was once your skin,
Casts on me, an embellish scar,
That at one time,
Bore nothing but your name!

17. Tastes of Sunlight!

The night is so dark
That I miss the sense of sunlight,
The sheer emptiness of the bright blue shining sky,
I long to see you again my beloved,
Because when I kiss you,
I taste sunlight on your skin.

18. The Morning Rainbow!

Rest your head on my chest
And sleep to the tune of my heartbeat
Let the murmurs of the winter breeze
Be silenced by the warmth of my chest,
Lay with me till sunlight shines
Across your face the next morning,
And turns you into a blazing mirage
Of a morning rainbow,
That appears when there is no raindrop in sight.

19. When I Write For Her

When I write for you, look deeply into the letters,
They contain in them,
The warmth of my blood, which runs through my veins,
Ever so fast,
Each time someone says your name.
Each time the sun sets in the red horizon,
When I walk beside you, close your eyes,
Fell the breath I take, a breath that is full of you,
A breath I wouldn't want to let go,
Each time I hold your hand,
Sense the tremble, of my soft fingers,
As they are afraid to touch and feel the comfort,
That they longed for,
Every moment I am with you, you need to know,
That I am yours!

20. You Would Never Know

A raging fire burns within me,
That would engulf and drag you
In from your very core,
And you would never know!
You would be mesmerised and pulled
Towards a dark deserted shore,
And you would never know!
You would tread across
an unknown land, curious and compelled.
And you would never know!
You would sink into the deepest trench
That would exist in your subconscious mind,
And you would never know
Stay away from my burning fire,
I warn you,
Because whatever the effect would be,
You would never know!

21. Strangers in Mirrors!

Someday I shall tell you of the secret of the fire within your
mirror.
Someday you shall see a reflection that is no longer strange,
Someday we shall stumble upon sobriety.
Till then Strangers we remain.

22. Sunshine and eternity

Sunshine and eternity
Life is how we dwell in the meadows of the dark lands,
Let sunshine walk amongst us and embalm our barren souls
with the warmth of happiness!
Let's turn to each other and smile with an awkward glee,
As Sunshine lets the dark night break it's fast with the wicked
smile of eternity!

23. Silence of the Quill

I want to write for me,
Of Those words that bleed within,
Of those noises that scream through my chest each night,
I fail to find them on my Palm,
Each time I hold my quill,
I see melancholy, on a blank piece of parchment,
Which reflects what lies inside me.

24. Will you be Mine?

If I write for you, will you be my poem,
If I stand by you, will you be my shadow,
If I smile for you, will you be my happiness,
If I wake up to you, will you be my sunshine ,
If I walk with you, will you be my footsteps ,
If I am with you, Will you be with me ?

25. Dreams of me

Dreams of me
Dream of me today,
Dreams that may erode from you the essence of every deep sleep
that u have had in your existence till date,
Dream of me today,
Dreams that may drop you through an unknown abyss and not
knowing where to go,
Dream of me today,
Until every pore of your skin screams out my name.
Dream of me today,
Until the morning rays wake up your senses as if they were born
just yesterday,
Dream of me today,
Until the calendar is void of days to go through for us again.

26. Written for you

When I write for you. Keep it with you,
someday when I'm gone,
You can open up that parchment,
And read through once more,
Years from when I'm gone,
You will know, what you meant for me ,
And how those words meant for you,
Some winters may pass, some summers may stay,
Some memories may remain,
And let me be one of them,
Memories of summer,
Written for you, by me , for us .

27. The Man & the Billboard

She looked at the shining billboard,

Mesmerised by the man as he sat and wrote,

She looked in awe and told her friends and foe,

How she wished to sit beside the man on the billboard,

And There I sat, in a corner under the stairs, watching her from

a distance,

Clenching a book, of all that I wrote for her,

Those pages she never once read,

Those pages she wouldn't see ever!

28. Soulmates and Soul Talk!

Seldom have we both realised we've built a world of our own.
A virtual world which is just us and two different hemispheres.
Every day we tread to the brink of each side and look across to
the other.
We know the other side better than our own.
Lest we forget to realise that you have my back and I have yours
and we continue looking over each other's shoulders.
Not turning back.
Never turning back at all.